CHECKERBOARD BIOGRAPHY LIBRARY

U.S. PRESIDENTS

The
United States Presidents

JAMES MONROE

ABDO Publishing Company

Megan M. Gunderson

Published by ABDO Publishing Company, 8000 West 78th Street, Edina, Minnesota 55439.
Copyright © 2009 by Abdo Consulting Group, Inc. International copyrights reserved in all
countries. No part of this book may be reproduced in any form without written permission from the
publisher. The Checkerboard Library™ is a trademark and logo of ABDO Publishing Company.

Printed in the United States.

Cover Photo: Corbis
Interior Photos: Alamy pp. 10, 11, 17, 19; AP Images pp. 5, 14; Corbis pp. 9, 12–13;
     Getty Images pp. 23, 25; iStockphoto pp. 29, 32; National Archives p. 27;
     Photo Researchers p. 15; Picture History pp. 16, 20

Editor: Heidi M.D. Elston
Art Direction & Cover Design: Neil Klinepier
Interior Design: Neil Klinepier

Library of Congress Cataloging-in-Publication Data

Gunderson, Megan M., 1981-
  James Monroe / Megan M. Gunderson.
       p. cm. -- (The United States presidents)
  Includes index.
  ISBN 978-1-60453-467-2
  1. Monroe, James, 1758-1831--Juvenile literature. 2. Presidents--United States--Biography--
Juvenile literature. I. Title.

  E372.G86 2009
  973.5'4092--dc22
  [B]
                              2008044332

CONTENTS

JAMES MONROE

James Monroe was the fifth president of the United States. He had a long political career before taking office. Today, his presidency is most remembered for the Monroe Doctrine.

Monroe grew up in Virginia. In 1774, he entered college. Two years later, he left school to fight in the **American Revolution**. Monroe fought bravely under General George Washington. After the war, he studied law.

In 1782, Monroe entered politics. He served in the Virginia House of Delegates, the Continental Congress, and the U.S. Senate. Monroe then traveled to Europe. He was minister to France and minister to Great Britain. In 1803, he signed the Louisiana Purchase.

Monroe went on to serve as governor of Virginia. Then, he became **secretary of state** under President James Madison. During the War of 1812, he also served as **secretary of war**.

In 1816, Monroe was elected president. He served two terms before retiring to Virginia. Monroe had a successful presidency. His time in office became known as the Era of Good Feelings.

TIMELINE

1758 - On April 28, James Monroe was born in Westmoreland County, Virginia.

1774 - Monroe entered the College of William and Mary in Williamsburg, Virginia.

1776 - Monroe left school to begin fighting in the American Revolution; on December 25, Monroe crossed the Delaware River with General George Washington.

1782 - Monroe was elected to the Virginia House of Delegates.

1783 - Monroe began serving in the Continental Congress.

1786 - On February 16, Monroe married Elizabeth Kortright.

1790 - Monroe was elected to the U.S. Senate.

1794 - Washington nominated Monroe minister to France.

1799 - Monroe was elected governor of Virginia.

1803 - In France, Monroe signed the Louisiana Purchase; he became minister to Great Britain.

1811 - Monroe became secretary of state under President James Madison.

1814 - On September 27, Monroe replaced John Armstrong as secretary of war during the War of 1812.

1816 - Monroe was elected the fifth president of the United States.

1820 - On March 6, Monroe signed the Missouri Compromise; Monroe was reelected president.

1823 - On December 2, Monroe gave a speech that outlined the Monroe Doctrine.

1830 - Elizabeth Monroe died on September 23.

1831 - On July 4, James Monroe died.

DID YOU KNOW?

During James Monroe's presidency, five new states joined the nation. Mississippi became a state in 1817. Illinois joined the United States in 1818, followed by Alabama in 1819. Maine became a state the next year, followed by Missouri in 1821.

In 1817, Monroe became the first president to travel by steamboat.

One of Monroe's classmates at Campbelltown Academy in Virginia was John Marshall. Marshall became chief justice of the U.S. Supreme Court in 1801. He served on the Court until 1835.

Monroe is not the only president to have died on the Fourth of July. Thomas Jefferson and John Adams both died on Independence Day in 1826.

VIRGINIA CHILDHOOD

James Monroe was born in Westmoreland County, Virginia, on April 28, 1758. At that time, Virginia was a British colony.

James had one sister and three brothers. He was the oldest son of Elizabeth Jones Monroe and Spence Monroe. Spence was a farmer and a carpenter.

At age 11, James began attending school. He went to Campbelltown Academy. There, James studied mathematics and Latin.

For fun, James liked to hunt small game birds. So, he often carried a rifle on his way to and from school. Many nights, James provided part of the family dinner!

In 1774, Spence Monroe died. As the oldest son, James was left in charge of the family property. Still, he was able to continue his education that July. He entered the College of William and Mary in Williamsburg, Virginia.

FAST FACTS

BORN - April 28, 1758

WIFE - Elizabeth Kortright (1768–1830)

CHILDREN - 3

POLITICAL PARTY - Democratic-Republican

AGE AT INAUGURATION - 58

YEARS SERVED - 1817–1825

VICE PRESIDENT - Daniel D. Tompkins

DIED - July 4, 1831, age 73

When James attended the College of William and Mary, Williamsburg was the capital of Virginia.

JOINING THE FIGHT

At the College of William and Mary, Monroe did not focus on his schoolwork. Instead, he listened to people speaking out against British rule. Monroe agreed that the colonies should break free from Britain.

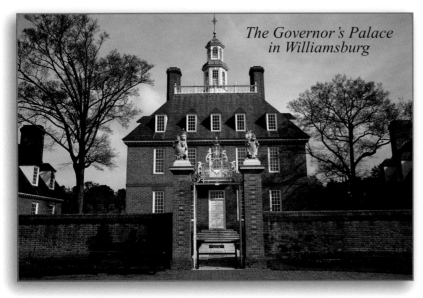

The Governor's Palace in Williamsburg

So, Monroe began participating in anti-British activities. He even joined his fellow students in **raiding** the British Governor's Palace. They stole 200 guns and 300 swords. Then, they presented the weapons to the Virginia **militia**!

In 1775, the **American Revolution** officially began. Monroe wanted to join the fight. So in 1776, he left college to join the

Continental army. He entered as a lieutenant in the Third Virginia **Regiment**.

Meanwhile, colonial leaders approved the Declaration of Independence on July 4, 1776. This paper declared the colonies "Free and Independent States." But, official separation from Great Britain would only be won through years of war. So, the fight for freedom continued.

In autumn 1776, Monroe fought battles in Harlem Heights and White Plains, New York. Then on December 25, he crossed the icy Delaware River with General George Washington. This famous crossing led to the Battle of Trenton in New Jersey.

Washington's forces captured Trenton from the British. But during the battle, Monroe was wounded. He was shot in the shoulder and nearly died. For his bravery, Monroe was promoted to captain.

After recovering, Monroe continued to serve under General Washington. He fought in two Pennsylvania battles in 1777. On September 11, Monroe fought in the Battle of the Brandywine.

In Emanuel Leutze's 1851 painting, Monroe holds the American flag as Washington leads his men across the Delaware River.

Then on October 4, he fought in the Battle of Germantown. The British won both battles. Still, Monroe was promoted to major.

Next, Monroe became **aide-de-camp** to General William Alexander. In this role, he suffered through the long winter at Valley Forge. The Continental army faced cold, disease, and starvation at this Pennsylvania camp. Yet the troops did not give up.

In summer 1778, Monroe again helped General Washington in New Jersey. He served as Washington's scout before the Battle of Monmouth. Soon afterward, Monroe left the military. He then returned to Williamsburg.

POLITICS AND FAMILY

Thomas Jefferson

In 1780, Monroe began studying law under Virginia governor Thomas Jefferson. The two became good friends. Along with James Madison, they worked together for many years.

Monroe was elected to the Virginia House of Delegates in 1782. Then in 1783, he began serving in the Continental Congress. This group served as the temporary U.S. government until 1789.

In Congress, Monroe fought for navigation rights on the Mississippi River. The river was under Spanish control. But, Monroe felt Americans should be able to use it for shipping goods.

Monroe also helped Jefferson write laws about developing America's western lands. Twice, Monroe traveled west to see these areas.

The American Revolution ended in 1783. That same year, Monroe entered the Continental Congress.

Elizabeth Monroe

While serving in Congress, Monroe met Elizabeth Kortright of New York. They married on February 16, 1786.

The Monroes later had two daughters. Eliza Kortright was born in 1787. Maria Hester followed in 1803. Their son, John Spence, died very young.

The Monroe family was close. Monroe believed education was important for girls as well as boys. So, Eliza and Maria were well educated for their time.

In 1786, Monroe retired from Congress. He and his wife then moved to Fredericksburg, Virginia. That year, Monroe became a lawyer and began practicing law.

Monroe was reelected to the Virginia House of Delegates in 1787. The next year, Virginia held a convention to approve the new U.S. **Constitution**.

Today, the James Monroe Museum and Memorial Library is in Fredericksburg, Virginia. Monroe's law office once stood on this site.

Monroe was concerned that the **Constitution** did not yet include a bill of rights. He also felt it gave the national government too much power over the states. So, Monroe voted against the Constitution. Still, the convention approved it.

After the U.S. Constitution was officially adopted, Monroe supported it. It established the U.S. Senate and the U.S. House of Representatives. Under this new government, Washington was elected the first president in 1789.

THE DIPLOMAT

Monroe was elected to the U.S. Senate in 1790. At the time, the **Federalist** Party controlled Congress. Monroe disagreed with the party's policies. So, he helped Jefferson and Madison form the **Democratic-Republican** Party in 1792.

Meanwhile, Great Britain and France were at war. The Federalists supported Britain. The Democratic-Republicans feared this would damage America's relationship with France. President Washington hoped having a Democratic-Republican minister to France would avoid this. So, he nominated Monroe in 1794.

At the time, the French were upset about the Jay Treaty. This was a trade agreement between the United States and Great Britain. France worried America was favoring Britain.

In France, Monroe did not defend the treaty. So, Washington felt Monroe was not representing his country properly. He asked Monroe to return from France.

Monroe arrived home in spring 1797. He then wrote a **pamphlet** attacking President Washington. It was published in December.

Monroe's anti-Washington pamphlet is titled A View of the Conduct of the Executive, in Foreign Affairs of the United States.

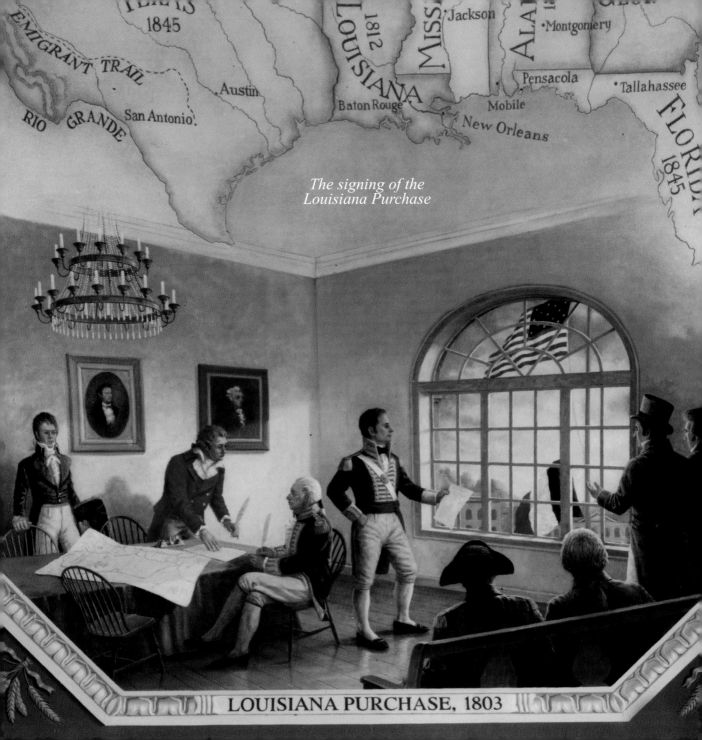

The signing of the
Louisiana Purchase

LOUISIANA PURCHASE, 1803

In 1799, Monroe was elected governor of Virginia. He served in this position until 1802. As governor, Monroe supported public education. He also promoted Jefferson for president in the election of 1800.

Jefferson became the third U.S. president in 1801. In January 1803, he decided to send Monroe back to France. The United States wanted to purchase New Orleans from France. This area of Louisiana was important to U.S. trade.

Monroe arrived in France on April 12. There, he assisted U.S. minister to France Robert Livingston. Monroe was surprised to learn France was willing to sell all of Louisiana. On May 2, Monroe and Livingston signed the Louisiana Purchase. This doubled the size of the United States.

Meanwhile, Monroe had been named minister to Great Britain. So in July, he went to London. At the time, Britain was seizing U.S. ships and forcing U.S. sailors into service. So, Jefferson had Monroe discuss possible solutions with the British.

The result was a treaty. Monroe signed it on December 31, 1806. However, Jefferson felt the treaty did not do enough to protect American ships. So he rejected it. Monroe then returned home in December 1807.

SECRETARY OF STATE

In spring 1810, Monroe was reelected to the Virginia House of Delegates. Then in January 1811, he began a new term as governor of Virginia. That November, he resigned to become **secretary of state** under President Madison.

At the time, the British were still attacking U.S. ships. Madison and Monroe felt war was necessary. So on June 18, 1812, Congress declared war on Great Britain. This was the beginning of the War of 1812.

In August 1814, the British captured Washington, D.C. President Madison blamed **Secretary of War** John Armstrong for not preventing the attack. So on September 27, he replaced Armstrong with Monroe. Now, Monroe held two **cabinet** positions at once!

On December 24, the United States and Great Britain signed the Treaty of Ghent. With this, the countries agreed to end the war. In March 1815, Monroe stepped down as secretary of war. He remained secretary of state for another two years.

Many people respected Monroe's leadership during the war. So in 1816, he ran for president. Monroe easily defeated **Federalist** Rufus King. He won 183 electoral votes to King's 34. Governor of New York Daniel D. Tompkins was elected vice president.

*Vice President
Daniel D. Tompkins*

PRESIDENT MONROE

Monroe was **inaugurated** the fifth U.S. president on March 4, 1817. The White House had been burned during the War of 1812. So, the Monroe family could not move in until September 1817. In the meantime, Monroe traveled around the nation. This helped Americans get to know their president.

When Monroe took office, there was trouble on the border between Georgia and Florida. At the time, Spain controlled Florida. Runaway slaves and Seminole Native Americans from Florida were attacking U.S. towns.

So, Monroe sent General Andrew Jackson to stop the attacks. Jackson invaded Florida. There, he fought what became known as the First Seminole War.

Secretary of State John Quincy Adams then organized a treaty with Spain. The Transcontinental Treaty was signed in 1819. In it, Spain agreed to give Florida to the United States. Spain also gave up any claims to the Oregon Territory. In exchange, the United States gave Spain the territory of Texas.

PRESIDENT MONROE'S CABINET

FIRST TERM
MARCH 4, 1817– MARCH 5, 1821

- **STATE** – John Quincy Adams
- **TREASURY** – William H. Crawford
- **WAR** – John C. Calhoun
- **NAVY** – Benjamin W. Crowninshield
  Smith Thompson (from January 1, 1819)
- **ATTORNEY GENERAL** – Richard Rush
  William Wirt (from November 15, 1817)

SECOND TERM
MARCH 5, 1821– MARCH 4, 1825

- **STATE** – John Quincy Adams
- **TREASURY** – William H. Crawford
- **WAR** – John C. Calhoun
- **NAVY** – Smith Thompson
  Samuel L. Southard (from September 16, 1823)
- **ATTORNEY GENERAL** – William Wirt

Meanwhile, Americans had begun arguing about slavery. So on March 6, 1820, President Monroe signed the Missouri Compromise.

The compromise admitted Maine as a free state and Missouri as a slave state. And, it banned slavery in the northern part of the Louisiana Territory. This kept a balance between slave and free states represented in the Senate. Temporarily, Americans on both sides of the slavery issue were satisfied.

Later that year, Monroe was reelected president. The next year, March 4 was a Sunday. So, Monroe was **inaugurated** on March 5, 1821.

During his second term, President Monroe gave one of his most famous speeches. In Congress on December 2, 1823, Monroe outlined what would become the Monroe Doctrine. At the time, the United States feared that Spain would try to reclaim some of its former colonies. And, the United States worried Russia wanted to take over land in northwestern North America. Monroe responded to these threats in his speech. He said North and South America were free. Europe should not try

SUPREME COURT APPOINTMENT

SMITH THOMPSON - 1823

to establish new colonies there. Also, he said the nation would see attacks on its neighbors as threats to the United States. In return, he promised not to interfere in European wars.

The Monroe Doctrine is one of the most important elements of Monroe's presidency. Long after he left office, U.S. presidents continued to follow its ideas.

The Monroe Doctrine came from the president's seventh annual address to Congress.

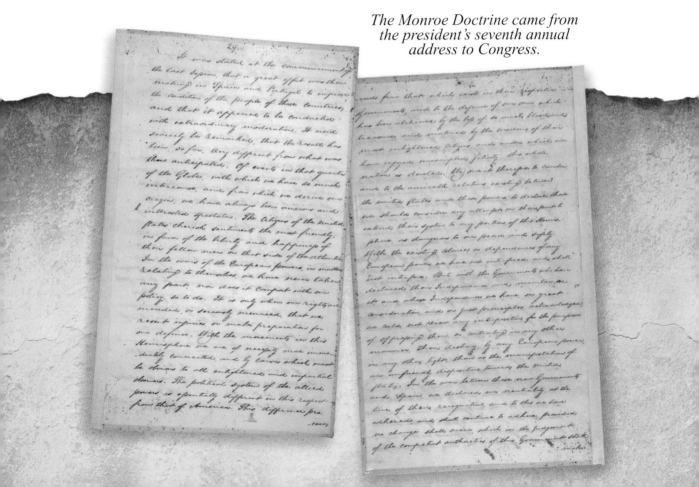

RETIREMENT

President Monroe decided not to run for a third term. So in 1824, three of his **cabinet** members ran for president! Secretary Adams won the election. **Secretary of War** John C. Calhoun was elected vice president.

In 1825, the Monroes retired to Leesburg, Virginia. Their new home was called Oak Hill. The following year, Monroe became a **regent** of the University of Virginia. Jefferson had founded this school in Charlottesville in 1819.

Monroe became president of Virginia's **constitutional** convention in 1829. There, he helped amend the state constitution. This was Monroe's last public office.

On September 23, 1830, Elizabeth Monroe died at Oak Hill. Monroe missed her very much. So that year, he sold his home and moved to New York City. He lived there with his daughter Maria while his health weakened. James Monroe died on July 4, 1831.

Monroe had a successful career in state and national politics. He helped with foreign relations as minister to France and minister to Great Britain. He continued this work as **secretary of state**.

As president, Monroe signed the Missouri Compromise. And, he introduced the Monroe Doctrine. James Monroe's contributions had a lasting effect on the United States.

Monroe's grave site in Richmond, Virginia

OFFICE OF THE PRESIDENT

BRANCHES OF GOVERNMENT

The U.S. government is divided into three branches. They are the executive, legislative, and judicial branches. This division is called a separation of powers. Each branch has some power over the others. This is called a system of checks and balances.

EXECUTIVE BRANCH

The executive branch enforces laws. It is made up of the president, the vice president, and the president's cabinet. The president represents the United States around the world. He or she oversees relations with other countries and signs treaties. The president signs bills into law and appoints officials and federal judges. He or she also leads the military and manages government workers.

LEGISLATIVE BRANCH

The legislative branch makes laws, maintains the military, and regulates trade. It also has the power to declare war. This branch consists of the Senate and the House of Representatives. Together, these two houses make up Congress. Each state has two senators. A state's population determines the number of representatives it has.

JUDICIAL BRANCH

The judicial branch interprets laws. It consists of district courts, courts of appeals, and the Supreme Court. District courts try cases. If a person disagrees with a trial's outcome, he or she may appeal. If the courts of appeals support the ruling, a person may appeal to the Supreme Court. The Supreme Court also makes sure that laws follow the U.S. Constitution.

Qualifications for Office

To be president, a person must meet three requirements. A candidate must be at least 35 years old and a natural-born U.S. citizen. He or she must also have lived in the United States for at least 14 years.

Electoral College

The U.S. presidential election is an indirect election. Voters from each state choose electors to represent them in the Electoral College. The number of electors from each state is based on population. Each elector has one electoral vote. Electors are pledged to cast their vote for the candidate who receives the highest number of popular votes in their state. A candidate must receive the majority of Electoral College votes to win.

Term of Office

Each president may be elected to two four-year terms. Sometimes, a president may only be elected once. This happens if he or she served more than two years of the previous president's term.

The presidential election is held on the Tuesday after the first Monday in November. The president is sworn in on January 20 of the following year. At that time, he or she takes the oath of office:

I do solemnly swear (or affirm) that I will faithfully execute the office of President of the United States, and will to the best of my ability, preserve, protect and defend the Constitution of the United States.

LINE OF SUCCESSION

The Presidential Succession Act of 1947 defines who becomes president if the president cannot serve. The vice president is first in the line of succession. Next are the Speaker of the House and the President Pro Tempore of the Senate. If none of these individuals is able to serve, the office falls to the president's cabinet members. They would take office in the order in which each department was created:

Secretary of State

Secretary of the Treasury

Secretary of Defense

Attorney General

Secretary of the Interior

Secretary of Agriculture

Secretary of Commerce

Secretary of Labor

Secretary of Health and Human Services

Secretary of Housing and Urban Development

Secretary of Transportation

Secretary of Energy

Secretary of Education

Secretary of Veterans Affairs

Secretary of Homeland Security

BENEFITS

- While in office, the president receives a salary of $400,000 each year. He or she lives in the White House and has 24-hour Secret Service protection.

- The president may travel on a Boeing 747 jet called Air Force One. The airplane can accommodate 70 passengers. It has kitchens, a dining room, sleeping areas, and a conference room. It also has fully equipped offices with the latest communications systems. Air Force One can fly halfway around the world before needing to refuel. It can even refuel in flight!

- If the president wishes to travel by car, he or she uses Cadillac One. Cadillac One is a Cadillac Deville. It has been modified with heavy armor and communications systems. The president takes Cadillac One along when visiting other countries if secure transportation will be needed.

- The president also travels on a helicopter called Marine One. Like the presidential car, Marine One accompanies the president when traveling abroad if necessary.

- Sometimes, the president needs to get away and relax with family and friends. Camp David is the official presidential retreat. It is located in the cool, wooded mountains in Maryland. The U.S. Navy maintains the retreat, and the U.S. Marine Corps keeps it secure. The camp offers swimming, tennis, golf, and hiking.

- When the president leaves office, he or she receives Secret Service protection for ten more years. He or she also receives a yearly pension of $191,300 and funding for office space, supplies, and staff.

PRESIDENTS AND THEIR TERMS

PRESIDENT	PARTY	TOOK OFFICE	LEFT OFFICE	TERMS SERVED	VICE PRESIDENT
George Washington	None	April 30, 1789	March 4, 1797	Two	John Adams
John Adams	Federalist	March 4, 1797	March 4, 1801	One	Thomas Jefferson
Thomas Jefferson	Democratic-Republican	March 4, 1801	March 4, 1809	Two	Aaron Burr, George Clinton
James Madison	Democratic-Republican	March 4, 1809	March 4, 1817	Two	George Clinton, Elbridge Gerry
James Monroe	Democratic-Republican	March 4, 1817	March 4, 1825	Two	Daniel D. Tompkins
John Quincy Adams	Democratic-Republican	March 4, 1825	March 4, 1829	One	John C. Calhoun
Andrew Jackson	Democrat	March 4, 1829	March 4, 1837	Two	John C. Calhoun, Martin Van Buren
Martin Van Buren	Democrat	March 4, 1837	March 4, 1841	One	Richard M. Johnson
William H. Harrison	Whig	March 4, 1841	April 4, 1841	Died During First Term	John Tyler
John Tyler	Whig	April 6, 1841	March 4, 1845	Completed Harrison's Term	Office Vacant
James K. Polk	Democrat	March 4, 1845	March 4, 1849	One	George M. Dallas
Zachary Taylor	Whig	March 5, 1849	July 9, 1850	Died During First Term	Millard Fillmore

PRESIDENT	PARTY	TOOK OFFICE	LEFT OFFICE	TERMS SERVED	VICE PRESIDENT
Millard Fillmore	Whig	July 10, 1850	March 4, 1853	Completed Taylor's Term	Office Vacant
Franklin Pierce	Democrat	March 4, 1853	March 4, 1857	One	William R.D. King
James Buchanan	Democrat	March 4, 1857	March 4, 1861	One	John C. Breckinridge
Abraham Lincoln	Republican	March 4, 1861	April 15, 1865	Served One Term, Died During Second Term	Hannibal Hamlin, Andrew Johnson
Andrew Johnson	Democrat	April 15, 1865	March 4, 1869	Completed Lincoln's Second Term	Office Vacant
Ulysses S. Grant	Republican	March 4, 1869	March 4, 1877	Two	Schuyler Colfax, Henry Wilson
Rutherford B. Hayes	Republican	March 3, 1877	March 4, 1881	One	William A. Wheeler
James A. Garfield	Republican	March 4, 1881	September 19, 1881	Died During First Term	Chester Arthur
Chester Arthur	Republican	September 20, 1881	March 4, 1885	Completed Garfield's Term	Office Vacant
Grover Cleveland	Democrat	March 4, 1885	March 4, 1889	One	Thomas A. Hendricks
Benjamin Harrison	Republican	March 4, 1889	March 4, 1893	One	Levi P. Morton
Grover Cleveland	Democrat	March 4, 1893	March 4, 1897	One	Adlai E. Stevenson
William McKinley	Republican	March 4, 1897	September 14, 1901	Served One Term, Died During Second Term	Garret A. Hobart, Theodore Roosevelt

PRESIDENT	PARTY	TOOK OFFICE	LEFT OFFICE	TERMS SERVED	VICE PRESIDENT
Theodore Roosevelt	Republican	September 14, 1901	March 4, 1909	Completed McKinley's Second Term, Served One Term	Office Vacant, Charles Fairbanks
William Taft	Republican	March 4, 1909	March 4, 1913	One	James S. Sherman
Woodrow Wilson	Democrat	March 4, 1913	March 4, 1921	Two	Thomas R. Marshall
Warren G. Harding	Republican	March 4, 1921	August 2, 1923	Died During First Term	Calvin Coolidge
Calvin Coolidge	Republican	August 3, 1923	March 4, 1929	Completed Harding's Term, Served One Term	Office Vacant, Charles Dawes
Herbert Hoover	Republican	March 4, 1929	March 4, 1933	One	Charles Curtis
Franklin D. Roosevelt	Democrat	March 4, 1933	April 12, 1945	Served Three Terms, Died During Fourth Term	John Nance Garner, Henry A. Wallace, Harry S. Truman
Harry S. Truman	Democrat	April 12, 1945	January 20, 1953	Completed Roosevelt's Fourth Term, Served One Term	Office Vacant, Alben Barkley
Dwight D. Eisenhower	Republican	January 20, 1953	January 20, 1961	Two	Richard Nixon
John F. Kennedy	Democrat	January 20, 1961	November 22, 1963	Died During First Term	Lyndon B. Johnson
Lyndon B. Johnson	Democrat	November 22, 1963	January 20, 1969	Completed Kennedy's Term, Served One Term	Office Vacant, Hubert H. Humphrey
Richard Nixon	Republican	January 20, 1969	August 9, 1974	Completed First Term, Resigned During Second Term	Spiro T. Agnew, Gerald Ford

PRESIDENTS 26–37, 1901–1974

PRESIDENT	PARTY	TOOK OFFICE	LEFT OFFICE	TERMS SERVED	VICE PRESIDENT
Gerald Ford	Republican	August 9, 1974	January 20, 1977	Completed Nixon's Second Term	Nelson A. Rockefeller
Jimmy Carter	Democrat	January 20, 1977	January 20, 1981	One	Walter Mondale
Ronald Reagan	Republican	January 20, 1981	January 20, 1989	Two	George H.W. Bush
George H.W. Bush	Republican	January 20, 1989	January 20, 1993	One	Dan Quayle
Bill Clinton	Democrat	January 20, 1993	January 20, 2001	Two	Al Gore
George W. Bush	Republican	January 20, 2001	January 20, 2009	Two	Dick Cheney
Barack Obama	Democrat	January 20, 2009			Joe Biden

"Peace is the best time for improvement and preparation of every kind." James Monroe

WRITE TO THE PRESIDENT

You may write to the president at:

**The White House
1600 Pennsylvania Avenue NW
Washington, DC 20500**

You may e-mail the president at:
comments@whitehouse.gov

GLOSSARY

aide-de-camp - a military officer who acts as an assistant to an officer with a higher rank.

American Revolution - from 1775 to 1783. A war for independence between Great Britain and its North American colonies. The colonists won and created the United States of America.

cabinet - a group of advisers chosen by the president to lead government departments.

constitution - the laws that govern a country or a state. The U.S. Constitution is the laws that govern the United States. Something relating to or following the laws of a constitution is constitutional.

Democratic-Republican - a member of the Democratic-Republican political party. During the early 1800s, Democratic-Republicans believed in weak national government and strong state government.

Federalist - a member of the Federalist political party. During the early 1800s, Federalists believed in a strong national government.

inaugurate (ih-NAW-gyuh-rayt) - to swear into a political office.

militia (muh-LIH-shuh) - a group of citizens trained for war or emergencies.

pamphlet (PAM-fluht) - a printed publication without a cover.

raid - to conduct a surprise attack.

regent - a member of a governing board.

regiment - a large military unit made up of troops.

secretary of state - a member of the president's cabinet who handles relations with other countries.

secretary of war - a member of the president's cabinet who handles the nation's defense.

WEB SITES

To learn more about James Monroe, visit ABDO Publishing Company on the World Wide Web at **www.abdopublishing.com**. Web sites about James Monroe are featured on our Book Links page. These links are routinely monitored and updated to provide the most current information available.

INDEX